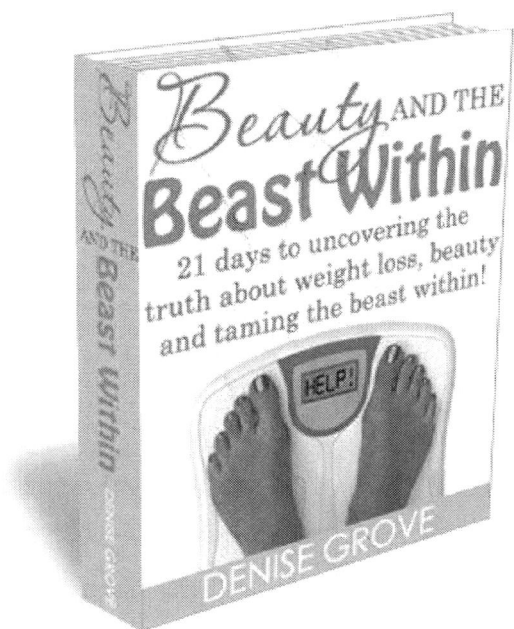

## NOTICE: You Do NOT Have the Right to Resell this Report!

# Beauty and the Beast Within

## Table of Contents

## About the Author

Denise Grove is wife to Greg, homeschooling mama to 7, grandma to 1, blogger, speaker, coffee drinker, dog lover, and all around crazy lady......desperately in love with Jesus.

Welcome to a glimpse of her life. It is a place where chaos abounds, tears are shed regularly, laughter is inevitable, and family is EVERYTHING!

She writes at choosingtoday.blogspot.com. She would love to connect with you. E-mail her at choosingtoday@msn.com or find her on twitter @choosingtoday.

## The Beautiful Woman's version of 1 Corinthians 13:1-8, 13

And now I will show you the most excellent way,

If I speak of calorie content and fat grams, but do not have love, I am only a resounding gong or a clanging cymbal.

If I have the gift of eating carrots instead of cake and can fathom all diet and exercise mantras, and if I have enough muscle mass that can move mountains, but do not have love, I am nothing.

If I give all my snacks to the poor and give over my body to the elliptical that I may boast, but do not have love, I gain nothing (ain't that the truth).

Love is patient, love is kind. It does not have perfectly manicured nails, it does not use concealer, it is not a size 0. It does not deprive itself, it is not self-destructive, it is not easily angered when its roots show, it keeps no record of food intake. Love does not delight in Botox but rejoices with the truth. It always protects, always trusts, always hopes, always perseveres. Love never fails.

But where there are skinny jeans, they will cease; where there are spinning classes, they will be stilled; where there is deprivation, it will pass away (and so might you)......

And now these three remain: faith, hope and love.

But the greatest of these is love.

# Introduction

*Though we travel the world over to find the beautiful,*
*we must carry it with us or we find it not.*

*~Ralph Wald Emerson*

Who wants to write a book on being beautiful? Maybe someone who has graced the cover of People magazine's "most beautiful people" issue or maybe someone who spends countless hours and money on appearing that way or maybe just maybe someone like me who is sick and tired of all the lies and misconceptions that have filled our brains and is sick and tired myself of trying to find "beautiful".

Now who wants to buy a book on being beautiful? Just about every woman I know. The teenager with the mouth full of braces and changing body, the 70 year old still buying the wrinkle cream and everyone in between. We all want to feel beautiful....be told we are beautiful and achieve perfection. The problem is more of us resemble a box not an hour glass.

This book is not going to be your typical 21 days to a better body or the 21 day diet. This book is going to be a book about balance. Some of you may turn the last page and be on the path to a healthier thinner you but for some of you, you will turn the last page and go sit down and have a piece of cake. See, beauty and the struggle with it goes far deeper than the outside appearance.

So some days are going to have us look deep within ourselves and some days are going to be about healthy changes that will affect our health and body size. Think Marilyn Monroe meets Mother Theresa. This journey will not be about achieving perfection but finding peace.

You see perfection is impossible to attain and even if we found some assemblance of it before we even got to enjoy it, it would be gone.

Peace on the other hand can be lasting. At the turn of the last page I hope that beast within is tamed. That you know your true worth and value and that beauty is about far more than outward appearance.

So what made me land on 21 days?

Well I have heard it said that it takes that long to form a habit. Even though I said this is not a book about being skinny, it is a book about making changes. Those changes occur through a small series of choices we make every day. We will start tackling some tough stuff like our thoughts because it has been said that our thoughts become our actions and our actions become our habits and our habits become our destiny.

Some days might be tough and you may want to give up. Some days will be light and fun and seem like nothing at all. But all of this together will redefine for you your beautiful. Please see this through to the end. I promise you will have a different perspective when it's over and I promise you that you will find beautiful I know this because it is already there just waiting to be discovered!

So grab yourself a pen, some note cards, and a journal and let's get started!

## Day 1 – What's your definition of beautiful?

*Everything has beauty, but not everyone sees it.*
*~Confucius*

So do you have your journal? If not DO NOT do what I would typically do and put the book down until I get a chance to go find a cute little journal with a matching pen. There is a name for that. Procrastination. So if you don't have your journal go get yourself a piece of paper and any writing utensil(I don't care if you have to go find one of your children's nubby little broken crayons….just go get something).

So here we are. Day 1. Oh the possibilities…..a clean slate. The perfect time to make all kinds of resolutions for how we want this book to be different. The problem is we make them and then by about 10 days in we fall back into our old ways. Traditions. Creatures of habit. Feeling like failures but also not feeling we can be different.

Well, today CAN be different if we approach it correctly with our God-goggles on not just viewing it through our own eyes. Over the next 21 days I am going to share something with you about change. It's all about "choices". With each small choice can come permanent change. That can be for the good or bad that is why we are going to be intentional to be sure we are choosing for the good.

Even though there will be an emphasis on weight loss and being healthy this can apply to almost any area of our life because I believe rooted in any need for weight loss is the root of some sort of stronghold (please don't misunderstand I know there can be medical reasons and no I have not been evaluated by the food and drug admin). And even if your struggle doesn't involve food it is rooted in a stronghold somewhere.

# Beauty and the Beast Within

If you picked up this book you have struggled to find peace within yourself and have struggled to find your beautiful.

Today in our journal we are going to set some goals but we are not going to stop there. We are then going to spend some time praying and asking ourselves why.

- Why is this my goal?
- What do I think it will bring me?

If our goals are way off (and God will let us know if they are) we are setting ourselves up to fail. These need to be realistic God-given goals. We also need to discover the "why" behind our choices. So ask God honestly why you make the goals you make if you're not sure.

When I started on my weight loss journey a few years ago my goal was to be a size 2. That's what I was in high school and I saw no reason I couldn't be there again. The problem was this goal was not realistic. I could be a size 2 if all I did was think about it. Exercise constantly. Eat next to nothing. Be miserable. That doesn't work. And here's the thing, I have been a size 2 and I have been a size 12 and everything in between and there is no more happiness when I am almost killing myself at size 2 then there is when I am hating how I look and feel at a larger size.

Hear me out on this. If you think losing a certain amount of weight is your answer to all your problems you are DEAD WRONG. It will not do a thing for you if you are still battling the stronghold of food or a stronghold of something else.

Yes food is just as much a stronghold when you are depriving yourself as when your are stuffing yourself. At a bigger size you just get a different result on the outside but misery still takes up residence in your heart either way.

If you think a certain amount of weight loss will make you happier, be more fulfilling, or make someone love you more you need to just stop right now. That would be the reason you failed before because you were looking for something out of it that it just cannot provide. Only God will fill those empty space and longings.

So what is a good goal for you? Do you know the number on the scale that is good and healthy for you? And I mean good and healthy not the stinking one you were in high school, not the one your best friend is and heaven knows not the one the world says you should be. The one you can maintain without obsessing.

I know mine and it's not a size 2 :) If you don't know then pray for God to help you set the goal that is right for you. The idea here is optimum health not to be a picture of what society has sold us. That is all a lie rooted in the father of lies himself. If he gets us focusing on that unrealistic goal he gets our focus off God. We will not allow that to happen!

After you have written some realistic goals I want you to go look at yourself in a mirror. Journal about what you see. Be honest and really write out what it is you think and feel when you look at yourself.

After you write about what you see and feel write down your definition of beautiful. Don't look it up just come up with your own definition. We are going to at the end of this journey take another look and I pray you will see yourself completely different.

Also today take one of your index cards and write the following verse on it:

*Do not conform any longer to the pattern of this world, but be transformed by the renewing of your mind. Then you will be able to test and approve what God's will is—his good, pleasing and perfect will. ~Romans 12:2*

# Beauty and the Beast Within

Start memorizing it! We are not going to conform any longer to the world and what it says we should look like but we are going to find God's will for our bodies and our life. Much of this battle will happen in our minds and we will fight the good fight by scripture memorization. This part WILL BE CRUCIAL. We will not succeed without it at least not long term.

Remember today to journal and pray. Today will be one of the toughest days. Hang with me here. Don't give up!

## Day 2 – Pray, Plan, Prioritize, and Put Into Action

*I praise you because I am fearfully and wonderfully made;*
*your works are wonderful, I know that full well.*

*Psalm 139:14*

Did you set some goals yesterday? How about the look and the mirror and the journaling assignment? Are the goals the same as last time you set goals or are they different? Did you pray about those goals and try to get to the bottom of why you want to achieve those things?

Whenever I set my goals, I know I then need to come up with a reasonable plan. When I need a reasonable plan to accomplish anything I have a system that came about because I am a procrastinator (have been as long as I can remember). I was the one who crammed for tests and waited until the night before a paper was due to write it.

This has its advantages and disadvantages. I used to look at it only in a negative light but I realized having the ability to put some things aside and just enjoy life has its advantages. Unfortunately if I put too much off and don't have a plan nothing gets accomplished. So this is what I learned to do:

1. Pray
2. Prioritize
3. Plan
4. Put it into action

I want God to order my "to do" list. I don't want the list to control me but be a guide. If God brings some unexpected thing my way today that is ok too.

His word is clear.....

*Commit to the Lord whatever you do, and your plans will succeed. ~Proverbs 16:3*
*In his heart a man plans his course, but the Lord determines his steps. ~Proverbs 16:9*

In learning to be healthier and find my beautiful I prayed and came up with a list.

So today we are going to make a list of things we can do to be healthier, happier, and possibly even thinner. It will look like this:

1. Drink more water
2. Eat a more balanced diet
3. Exercise more
4. Get more rest
5. Find an encouragement partner (I will explain more about this later)
6. Allow God to fill me
7. Be realistic

Grab your journal and write it down. Now look at it. Not rocket science. I don't have a PHD in nutrition sciences or the physiology. Just about everything we do over the next 20 days will fall under one of these categories.

# Beauty and the Beast Within

Our plan and priority today is to evaluate our water intake lately. This is the action step we are taking today. I know I want to eat my calories not drink them. Most drinks are nothing but empty calories. Just keeping ourselves hydrated by drinking pure water can combat many health and weight issues.

**So how much water are we going to drink?**

Take your weight and divide it by 2. That number is the number of ounces of water we are going to shoot for.  If you are not used to drinking water than just start with 60 to 80 ounces daily.  Sometimes I cut up lemon wedges and add to my water for a bit of flavor but other than that I drink just plain old water.  It is our body's most basic need yet most of us never get enough and it's not because it is not available to us.

It may seem like a lot if you aren't used to drinking that much but you can get used to it and you will feel a whole lot better. Try to drink most of it by late afternoon so you aren't up all night going to the bathroom.

**So what's your plan for more water drinking?**

A cute water bottle?

Getting some lemons?

Praying like a mad woman because you don't like water because you're a soda girl?

Whatever it is don't wait.  We are putting this one into action today!

Also in your journal write a prayer of praise thanking Him that we are fearfully and wonderfully made (Psalm 139) and asking for Him to help you in your quest to drink the amount of water you need in order to keep yourself as healthy as possible.

He created our bodies to need water and He provides this for us. Also thank Him for His provision of good, safe, clean drinking water and pray for those who struggle to have this very basic need.

Sometimes taking the focus off ourselves and putting it on to someone less fortunate makes our goal much more manageable. It is hard to complain about drinking water when I think of the small child who has none.

Keep memorizing Romans 12:2.

## Day 3 – Slow Down!

*"Death is nature's way of telling you to slow down"*

*-Anonymous*

Sometimes I swear I live life faster than the spin cycle on a washing machine. I walk fast. I talk fast. I read fast. At the moment I can't think of anything I don't do at top speed. We are busy people. We have 50 hours worth of stuff to do and only 24 hours in a day to do it.

Of all the things I do fast one of my worst habits is I eat fast! When I sit down to eat I often realize I am eating it so fast. Like it was my last meal or I had to catch a train or something. It is then that I think about how much I take for granted. All the food I have and I don't take a lot of time to enjoy it and be thankful for it.

Often times we eat fast and we keep eating because we haven't given our body a chance to realize we are full. Today we are going to choose to SLOW DOWN!

Take some time and ask yourself before you get more **"am I still hungry?"**

This is our priority today that we will put into action. Now that doesn't mean water won't be a priority. It is. We are going to keep building on this foundation of good choices.

I know this is tough especially because we spend so much of our time on the go. But I promise you that you will eat less and your body will thank you because the slower you eat and the more you chew the easier it is on your digestive system. There is scientific proof that eating fast and obesity are linked to one another.

And if food is not your issue what is the thing you are stuffing in at a rapid pace? Is it your quiet time or time invested in a relationship? Or are you trying to "fill" up on material things that you think will satisfy?

Today we are going to journal and thank God that He is the only one who truly satisfies. Also, ask Him to help you to slow down and realize when you are full. Praise Him that He has provided you with so much and ask Him to help you be content when you have had enough.

Remember Romans 12:2 because this is your last day to memorize it. We will be getting a new verse tomorrow!

## Day 4 – Who Do You Think is Beautiful?

*Charm is deceptive, and beauty is fleeting;*
*but a woman who fears the LORD is to be praised*

*Proverbs 31:30*

Get out your journal today and list 10 women you think are beautiful. After each of their names tell why you think this about them. I know whenever I think about a beautiful woman it really never starts with appearance.

In fact isn't it interesting that the Bible never mentions a person's BMI or counting calories or nutrition information. In all of Jesus' teaching he never mentions weight or the need to be thin. He talks about following Him. He talks about serving one another and loving our enemies.

The chick in Proverbs 31 is never once described by her appearance, her outward beauty but by her actions. Her husband has confidence in her, she works hard, she provides for her family, she helps the poor and needy, she speaks with wisdom and her clothing are strength and dignity not Chanel.

Are you getting my point here?

When her children rise up and call her blessed it will be because of her actions not because of her ability to wear skinny jeans or her perfectly manicured nails. We won't be remembered for these things. It is our actions that make us beautiful. Outward beauty is fleeting.

Did you hear me?

# Beauty and the Beast Within

It will be gone someday….no amount of Botox will hang onto it, no amount of anything and you wouldn't be remembered for it if it did.

Please do not misunderstand me. I paint my nails and if I had the money they would have acrylic on them. My hair is not naturally blonde (well duh) and I love to shop. My point is when all of that becomes my only focus and I forget about all the actions that Christ talked about my life starts to get out of balance and an out of balance life is an unhappy life.

Not only do I want you to journal about the beautiful people you know but also about what you want to remembered for. You see when I start to get out of control on this vanity thing and I start to feel a little insane because it is hard to keep a perfect appearance.

Repeat after me….

*Vanity can become insanity.*

Say it one more time….

*Vanity can become insanity.*

It is not what I want people to remember about me!

List all the things you want to be remembered for and see how much of your list consists of things involving your outward appearance. Be a certain weight is not going to be the thing people say about me when I am gone. Nor do I want it to be.

After you have done that get another index card and start memorizing Proverbs 31:30:

*Charm is deceptive, and beauty is fleeting; but a woman who fears the LORD is to be praised.*

It is not a long verse so we will only have today to have it ingrained into our pretty little heads and then we will learn something new!

Don't forget keep drinking your water. If you are not up to drinking as much as you should be increase it a few ounces each day until you hit your goal and also don't forget to SLOW down!

## Day 5 – Lies, Lies, and More Lies!

*Once your soul has been enlarged by a truth,*
*it can never return to its original size.*

*~Blaise Pascal*

I hate being lied to….don't you?  Yet we believe lies on a daily basis about ourselves and don't usually stop once for even a second to question if what we believe is true. Today we are going to spend some time in God's word.

I want you to write down 10 statements about yourself and 10 statements about beauty in your journal and then I want you to search God's Word to see if they are true.

For example at one time "I am stupid" would have been on my list.  Every time I would slip up on a diet or mess something up I would tell myself that I was stupid.  Well if I were to search God's Word  I would find out that I was fearfully and wonderfully made (psalm 139) and that I have been given the mind of Christ(1 Corinthians 2).  See I was believing a lie.

In order to know the truth we need to search it out for ourselves then we need to believe it even when we don't feel like it.  2 Corinthians 10:4-5  tells us that we are to take every thought captive and make it obedient to Christ and that we have been given divine power to do so.  In fact that is a good one to remember so get out your index card and write it down:

*The weapons we fight with are not the weapons of the world. On the contrary, they have divine power to demolish strongholds.  We demolish arguments and every pretension that sets itself up against the knowledge of God, and we take captive every thought to make it obedient to Christ. ~ 2 Corinthians 10:4-5*

# Beauty and the Beast Within

After you write your statements and find out if they are true or not I want you to write something else in your journal that has helped me when I couldn't figure out how to take all those lies captive:

**C** - Cease Activity - get alone and get quiet!

**A** - Apply God's word - you gotta know it to apply it so study it faithfully

**P** - Persevere past what you're feeling and Praise God in the midst of it

**T** - Talk out loud - God's word is powerful especially when spoken out loud

**I** - Involve others - don't try to do this alone

**V** - Voice the victory - praise God for all your victories big and small

**E** - Evaluate for next time

These are the steps I would take to take all my thoughts captive and to stop believing the lies. I hope that helps you and I hope today you start to uncover the lies you have been believing about yourself and true beauty!

## Day 6 – Move More!

*The only exercise some people get is jumping to conclusions,
running down their friends, side-stepping responsibility,
and pushing their luck!*

*~Author Unknown*

Well we talked about motives, water, and slowing down. How's it going so far??? I hope it hasn't been too painful.

I bet today's title already seems a bit painful. I know what you are thinking. You are thinking that I am going to tell you some complicated exercise routine or tell you to buy some expensive equipment. Rest assured I am not. Pretty much everything I tell you is not going to cost anymore than the cost of this book.

When I lost weight I started walking. It was that simple. No gym membership or expensive equipment just my own two feet and the open road. I eventually worked up to some running but walking is still my favorite. I never did get that runner's high.
I know it sounds simple but this whole weight thing isn't that complicated. Move more, eat less. I keep repeating that to myself every day. Move more and eat less! Set an exercise goal today. I suggest you get a pedometer. They are fairly inexpensive. See how many steps you take each day and try increasing it little by little.

Find a walking partner if you can and when you do go alone or if you don't have a partner spend the time in prayer or download some good praise music or the Bible on your Ipod.

Start by trying a mile and then increase it as you feel like you can. Try to walk briskly. Change your pace and route often so your body doesn't become used to it.

In your journal thank God that He created you so perfectly. Thank Him for the ability to move. Pray that He helps you find time to move more this week! We don't have to do any of this alone. We do have His help!

And did you memorize 2 Corinthians 10:4-5???? I hope so. If not keep working on that one and when you have it down move on to this one. His Word is alive and active. It is our life and breath. Today let's start working on this one:

*Forget the former things; do not dwell on the past. See, I am doing a new thing! Now it springs up; do you not perceive it? I am making a way in the desert and streams in the wasteland. ~Isaiah 43:18-19*

We are going to stop dwelling on past failures and challenges. We are going to start looking for the "new thing" God wants to do in us and through us! We are going to stop with the excuses and we will move more. God will help us find the time and energy if we desire to do so. Our body is His temple so I know it is a request that he will honor!

Action Steps:

- ➢ Water
- ➢ Slow down
- ➢ Move more

## Day 7 – I'm Not Alone!

*The most terrible poverty is loneliness,*
*and the feeling of being unloved.*

*~Mother Teresa*

Do you ever feel lonely? Often times our weight is something that isolates us. We were meant for relationships but we use our insecurities as a wall we hide behind. We believe the lie that we can do this thing alone and that we don't need anyone.

Well the truth is we were created for relationship. We need support. We need friendship. We need someone to say "you can do it" and "I believe in you".

So today I want you to think of someone you can ask to pray for you for the remaining days we have left together on this journey. This might be difficult for you. You will have to be willing to drop the mask and be vulnerable with someone in your life. Although this is the shortest day it may prove to be the most difficult.

In your journal today write down the name of who you will ask to be your "encouragement partner" and then pick up the phone and ask them to support you in this journey.

If you are hesitant pray to God and ask Him to give you the courage to do this. Don't just think you can skip this part and go it alone. I will be checking tomorrow to see if you did this! And if you truly have no one then please e-mail me and I will pray for you.

Keep memorizing scripture and renewing your mind!

## Day 8– I Ate What?

*I love food and feel that it is something that should be enjoyed.
I eat whatever I want. I just don't overeat.*

*~Tyra Banks*

Did you get an encouragement partner? If not do not take one more step until you do.

The next two days are going to probably be the biggest pain to you. Not because what we will be doing is difficult to do but it will be a bit time consuming but please stick with me here. Step one will be to get yourself baggies. That's what I call 'em maybe you call 'em Ziplocs. Either way get some.

Even though it was a bit time consuming I learned to measure everything. I had to memorize it but after a while it just became a lifestyle. So take a baggie and just start counting out whatever you are going to eat into a serving size. Now obviously I am talking about snacks, cereal, etc....I don't expect you to put your chicken and rice into a baggie.

I promise you will be amazed at what one serving looks like. We aren't going to be counting calories here but we are going to become more aware of what a portion is.

It blew me away that I would sit down and easily consume 4 or 5 servings of something when I ate it out of the package.

If you live in a house like mine you can take all your baggies of food and put them into a container with a sign that says, "Mom's snacks - DO NOT TOUCH!"

The point is we mindlessly consume way too much and we are going to learn a little thing that isn't so popular today and that is moderation. I don't believe you should ever have to give anything up but it should never master you. Eat one serving of chips and one serving of cereal in your bowl.

We will talk about step 2 tomorrow.

Keep memorizing your scripture and journal today about the "new thing" God is doing in your life, maybe it will be teaching us about moderation. Pour out your heart to Him and let Him know your desires but also that you know that His ways are higher than your ways and you look forward to the divine plans He has for your life.

## Day 9 – I Want My Cake and Want To Eat It Too (all of it!)

*Inside some of us is a thin person struggling to get out,*
*but they can usually be sedated with a few pieces of chocolate cake.*

*~Author Unknown*

I tend to take things to the extreme when it comes to eating. I noticed patterns when I was in my weight loss journey. I wanted my cake and I wanted to eat ALL of it or I didn't want any and I was going to be miserable. It really doesn't work that way.

My tip for today is to take a few days and write some things down. For the next three days or so write down everything you put in your mouth.

After those three days think about where things would go wrong. What were you doing at the time? Where you bored or stressed?

This is a bit of a pain but one of two things will happen. You will either be very good about what you eat because you know it will be written down or you will eat like you honestly have been lately and you will begin to see patterns or maybe places where you were prone to extremes. Either way it will benefit you. You will either get to the root of why you're eating gets messed up or you will eat really well for three days and you will see that you can do it and you won't starve to death.

Often when we eat during the day we don't really realize how much we are eating. It is a bite here and a handful of something there. When it's written down we see it in black and white and we can often learn to catch those bad habits. Also this is where learning true portions sizes really helps us.

In your journal ask God to help you with this discipline over the next few days. Ask Him to help you see where you are prone to extremes.

Are you still working on Isaiah 43:18-19? I hope so. We are pouring truth into our minds. Nothing on this journey will be more important.

**Action steps so far:**

- ➢ Water
- ➢ Move more
- ➢ Portions
- ➢ Food journal
- ➢ Memorize scripture

Just because we are doing something new doesn't mean we stop doing what we have learned so far.  We are building a foundation for a healthier life.

## Day 10 - Wait, Wait, and Wait Some More!

*I say to myself, "The LORD is my portion;*
*therefore I will wait for him."*

*Lamentations 3:24*

Everything doesn't have to be instant. We can wait. I know that concept can be very foreign to us but it is possible and most often it is a reality. The weight may take us a month or even a year to lose.

That is ok!

We don't need to become discouraged and start stuffing ourselves. The only thing you should ever be stuffed to overflowing with is God himself. He is our portion. When we have eaten our sensible portion of food we just need to walk away and say "God thank you that you are my portion and that you have provided me with what I need to live and be healthy". And then wait. And wait. And wait.....knowing that it is God's desire for you to be healthy and also knowing that He might have very different ideas about your optimum weight than you do.

So what are we going to do today?

Stop, Pray, & Wait!

Now I know you might be asking what do I do while I wait (ok maybe you weren't asking but I will tell you anyway)…

While we are waiting, no matter what we are waiting for, we can be praying and also have a:

**W** - Willful Obedience

**A** – Anticipating an answer

**I** – Involving others and…

**T** – Thanking Him

You see just because we are waiting doesn't mean we can't be active. We need to still be willfully obeying Him. In that obedience we can also take Him at His word and know that he will provide an answer to our prayers(just remember it might night be His will for you to be built like a supermodel).

We can also be involving others in our prayers, in our struggles, and in our victories. We were never meant to go this life alone. Finally, while we are waiting we can thank Him for each and every moment we get through on this journey knowing that any victory big or small is because of Him!

Today in your journal thank Him for that very thing. Ask Him for patience in this weight loss walk. Ask Him for total surrender to the whole food thing or whatever else you feel you are in bondage to.

Keep memorizing Isaiah 43:18-19 today is the last day for that one we will learn a new one tomorrow.

P a g e | 31

## Day 11– Slow and Steady

*A handful of patience is worth more than a bushel of brains.*
*~Dutch Proverb*

I know we already talked about waiting yesterday but I thought we would spend today thinking about what makes that so hard for us. Sometimes we need to intentionally examine some things in our life so that it becomes more than just a bunch of head knowledge. If we want this to be a true permanent change in our life than it will take time and we will need to do a bunch of evaluation. We want our head knowledge to finally penetrate our hearts.

Slow and steady girls.

That is our goal. I know we live in a society that is "instant" but if you haven't figured it out yet weight loss is not. 1 to 2 pounds a week should be your goal and that means if you lose 2 pounds one week it is not the end of the world if you don't lose any the next.

The slower and more steady it comes off the better chance you will have at keeping it off. I love Biggest Loser. It is probably my favorite TV show but it IS NOT realistic. A 15-20 pound weight loss in a week is insane and hard to maintain.

So the next time you feel like you are frustrated because this is taking longer than you wanted it to remember this way it can be a permanent weight loss. You can stop being a yo-yo.

Beauty and the Beast Within

New verse:

*He gives strength to the weary and increases the power of the weak. Even youths grow tired and weary, and young men stumble and fall; but those who hope in the*

*LORD will renew their strength. They will soar on wings like eagles; they will run and not grow weary, they will walk and not be faint.*
*~Isaiah 40:29-31*

Now get it onto an index card and then get it into your heart. Do not stop memorizing scripture until it penetrates down into the marrow of your bone. It is life giving and life transforming.

Journal tonight about the times you feel most discouraged. Especially when the weight doesn't feel like it's coming off nearly as fast as it came on. Thank Him that He will give you strength. We will run and not grow weary!

## Day12 – Old Habits Die Hard

*"First we form habits then they form us.*
*Conquer your bad habits, or they'll eventually conquer you."*

*~Dr. Rob Gilbert*

Guess what? Sometimes I eat Dunkin Donuts for supper. I guess that is what I want to talk to you about today. Life is crazy. Sometimes we are traveling and we need a quick option for a meal. Don't beat yourself up or starve yourself. Eat the dang food for pity sakes.

It is not a once in a while trip through the drive through window that makes us overweight. It is the daily choices we make and the bad habits we form. When I do eat fast food I do try to make better choices. Like when I go to McDonalds with my kids I get a happy meal and I am fully satisfied when I am finished. I don't feel deprived by eating it and I don't deprive myself by not eating anything.

Moderation, everything in moderation!

I think Paul said it best:

**"Everything is permissible for me"--but not everything is beneficial. "Everything is permissible for me"--but I will not be mastered by anything. ~1 Corinthians 6:12**

Copy that on an index card. Write it, read it, and meditate on it.

Just don't be mastered by the thing!!!!! Another bad habit I learned to kick on a regular basis was eating after 6:00 pm. This doesn't mean I never did. By all means if you go out for ice-cream with your kiddos after 6:00 pm please have fun with them and eat your ice-cream.

But on a regular basis after you eat your last meal of the evening try not to snack a bunch before bed. It doesn't benefit us on our weight loss journey or aide in digestion. Much of our indigestion and reflux could be eliminated if we stopped eating late at night. Find things to do that make eating hard like reading a good book or painting your nails.

Tonight in your journal ask God to help you clearly distinguish between what is beneficial and what is not. Ask Him to help you that you are not mastered by anything. Pray about the habits you have formed.

Are they good?
Are they beneficial?
Does something need to go?

Sometimes it is hard to let go but we can do it not in our own strength but in His. We are not in this alone. He is there to help us and strengthen us all we have to do is cry out to Him!

Keep memorizing scripture we will be learning a new one tomorrow.

Action steps:

➢ Water
➢ Scriptures(our living water)
➢ Move more
➢ Slow down
➢ Be patient

You get the idea….don't stop building the foundation!

# Day 13 – Simple Exchanges and If You Get Down....Get Back Up!

*"Our greatest glory is not in never failing,*
*but in rising up every time we fail."*

*~ Ralph Waldo Emerson*

We are about half way through our journey. Have you felt like giving up yet? I am sure there have been good days and bad days. The biggest thing that will help you reach your goal and maintain any amount of weight loss will be the idea that if you mess up it does not need to define you or mean that you should give up because you are a failure.

That is a trick that Satan uses to get us to give up. In fact it is a trick Satan uses to get us to live in defeat over anything. A bad day just means you have an opportunity for tomorrow to be different. His mercies are new EVERY morning or better yet a slip up in our routine means we have the opportunity for the next moment to be different. His mercies can be new every moment.

Something you can do to help there not to be so many slip ups is to have some things on hand that you can substitute or exchange for your favorite snacks.

I substituted all sorts of things when I started losing weight. I swapped a "100 calorie" pack of cookies for the Oreos I love. I swapped Skinny Cow ice cream for Ben and Jerry's. I went to baked pita chips instead of regular chips.

Now more than ever there are plenty of things you can find to substitute for things you like. The key to making this work though is once again...moderation. You can only eat one pack of the cookies not 5. You can have one serving of the ice cream not 3 and for pity sakes don't sit down and eat the whole bag of pita chips.

This doesn't mean that I don't ever eat real Oreos. It just means for the most part I can find things to swap and save a bunch of calories and still enjoy what I am eating.

In your journal ask God to help you to crave healthy things. Give your cravings over to Him. Ask Him once again to help you to learn self-control. We have the Holy Spirit ladies. We are not alone in this.

How has the scripture memory going? I know I said it before but it so worth repeating......This will be the most significant thing you do over the next 21 days. If you learn nothing else you will have gained several new truths and His Word DOES NOT return void. You are renewing your mind day by day. So get out another index card and write the following:

**Taste and see that the LORD is good; blessed is the one who takes refuge in him.
Psalm 34:8**

Oh yes girls....He is good. All of the time! This is a short one so get it ingrained into your minds today because tomorrow we learn something new! It isn't hard. Write it, say it, and post it around where you will see it throughout the day!

## Day 14 - Sleeping Beauty

*A good laugh and a long sleep are the best cures in the doctor's book.*

*~Irish Proverb*

Today I have one word for you: SLEEP! And do it for at least 7 to 8 hours every night. I know it can be tempting to stay up late after you put the kiddos to bed but it has many adverse effects on our bodies including our overall health and immune system, our strength, our ability to think clearly, and you guessed it our weight.

There have been plenty of studies done linking lack of sleep and unhealthy weight gain. I go to bed by 10:00 almost every night. Rest has many benefits and you can find plenty in the Bible on this topic. We all need some down time. Now if you have a newborn or some other circumstance that inhibits you from proper sleep other than t.v, books, and hobbies then just know it is just a season and a season of rest will be coming soon.

Here is a little acrostic I came up with to help you remember the benefits:

**R** - Restores Us

**E** - Energizes Us

**S** - Soothes Us

**T** - Teaches Us

So grab yourself a new 3x5 card and start memorizing this verse:

*My soul finds rest in God alone; my salvation comes from him. He alone is my rock and my salvation; he is my fortress, I will never be shaken. ~Psalm 62:1-2*

In your journal thank Him that in Him our souls find rest. Ask Him to help you prioritize and organize your life in a way that you get the rest you need.

Thank Him that in Him you will NEVER be shaken! And while your at it ask Him to give you things throughout the day to make you laugh. We need to be joyful girls and I can tell you nothing can zap our joy like a poor body image and living in perpetual deprivation.

Pray scripture. Journal scripture. Speak scripture out loud. It is powerful!

And here are some things I hope make you laugh…

- I know what Victoria's Secret is. The secret is that nobody older than 30 can fit into their stuff.
- The Garlic Diet: You don't lose weight; you just look thinner from a distance.
- And finally….the older you get, the tougher it is to lose weight because by then, your body and your fat are really good friends.

You get the picture now go have a good laugh and get some rest!

## Day 15 – Letting Go

*"When one door closes another door opens;*
*but we so often look so long and so regretfully upon the closed door,*
*that we do not see the ones which open for us."*

*~ Alexander Graham Bell*

I love the start of a new Bible study. There isn't anything like getting together with those ladies and studying God's word. One of my favorites I have done on more than one occasion was "Breaking Free" by Beth Moore.

I learned so much from that study and each time I realized that there were things in my life that I needed to let go of.

If we are going to continue in the process of growing deeper with God it will always be a continual process of letting other things go and grabbing hold of Him.

Our weight is no different. If we are going to make this a permanent lifestyle change and not just a passing diet then some things will need to go. We have talked about a lot of them so far. We need to get into our minds that we are not on a diet but on a journey to be healthy. The point of all we have been doing so far is not so you can attain some ridiculous goal and then go back to the old lifestyle.

But please be aware one of the biggest things I needed to let go of was my goal and what I thought it would bring me. I had to let go of the idea that I was defined by my weight. I am not. I had to let go of the fact that I cannot realistically maintain that goal and my sanity. I had to let go of the lies I have believed and replace them with truth. I had to let go of my twisted idea of beauty and truly seek to become more like Jesus thus becoming more beautiful without one minute of Pilates or crunches.

# Beauty and the Beast Within

Get out an index card because I have a new verse for you to memorize....

*It is for freedom that Christ has set us free. Stand firm, then, and do not let yourselves be burdened again by a yoke of slavery. ~ Galatians 5:1*

We will only spend today on this one but please find time to write, say it, and meditate on it.  This is an important one.

Once you get through all the steps to a new healthier you be determined to not become a slave again to your old ways. We don't need to be in bondage to our weight or to food or to a twisted definition of beautiful. It is for freedom that Christ set us free!

In your journal think about what freedom means. What would freedom in the area of weight loss look like to you? What about freedom from the bondage of food? What if we just saw it as a means to be healthy and didn't constantly need to fixate on it.

Turn your thoughts into a prayer to God asking Him to set your free once and for all when it comes to dieting and weight. Also ask Him to help you redefine your beautiful in light of who He is and what He has done for you.

## Day 16 – No Bondage....Ok?

*Two kids went into their parents bathroom and noticed the weigh scale in the corner. "Whatever you do," cautioned one youngster to the other, "Don't step on it!"*

*"Why not?" asked the sibling.*

*"Because every time mom does, she lets out an awful scream!"*

I need to add a disclaimer today. You know yourself better than anyone. If what you read today you know will become bondage for you then don't give it another thought and move on.

Did you hear me? Move on!

I struggled if I should share what I am about to share but this helped me and I am trying to help you so I am going to share it.

Get yourself a decent scale and weigh yourself regularly. Now I don't mean to become obsessive about it but you really need to know. It is much easier to catch a five pound weight gain than a 15 or 20 pound weight gain. Skinny people know what they weigh and how their clothes fit.

After you have a scale you need to figure out your healthy weight. Notice I said healthy weight. Not dream weight. Not what you weighed when you were 10. Not the number that would cause you to become crazy and obsessed and unhappy. But the number that has you healthy and most importantly the number God has for you so that you can concentrate on Him and the plans He has not being distracted by some unachievable number.

Once you reach your number. Notice again I said YOUR number not your neighbor's number and not the number of the chic on the cover of the magazine but your number. Once you have that give yourself 5 pounds either way.

If you dip under know that in order to stay healthy you need to eat. If you go over it is time to be a bit more careful.

Get a good scale not the one that used to be in your grandmas bathroom. They are fairly inexpensive. And put it in a place where you will remember to get on. At first you may feel discouraged at the number and not want to get on but as you start making healthy changes and the number starts to go down it will be exciting.

I get on a few times a week first thing in the morning. I don't suggest you wait until later in the day after you've eaten at the local all you can eat buffet. Does anyone out there besides Lancaster County have smorgasbords? Who came up with that anyway?

If you can get on a few times a week to just check progress and keep an eye on where you are then this will be helpful to you. If you get on and then step off feeling depressed and defeated then throw the dang thing out the window. None of this is about defeat. If I make you feel bad, defeated, or worthless at any time then you have missed the point and you don't know my heart. God created us in all shapes and sizes and He makes no mistakes.

I have read varied thoughts on this topic and I am just sharing what worked for me. Please take or leave anything in this book to make it work for you. Also, I know I have touched on this before but it is worth repeating….

If you have a bad day or few days it doesn't mean you're a failure and you should give up totally on your weight loss goals. Just get back up. Don't give up. We are so quick after we eat that piece of cake to say I messed up I might as well eat the whole cake.

It is a bad mentality to have. One bad choice doesn't make a failure out of you. One bad day or even week on the scale does not need to define you.

You will have a bad day or days depending on the time of the month. That's ok just try to learn from it but keep going. You don't have to throw in the towel. You can make better choices tomorrow. You are not doomed. Satan would love to have you believe all these lies but remember we are combating lies with the truth of God's word.

Today in your journal talk to God about your feelings of failure in the past. Ask Him to help you to see yourself as He sees you through eyes of grace. Also turn your writing into a prayer for God to help you know your number. Ask Him to give you the strength to keep going even when you don't like what you see. Thank Him that He loves you just where you're at right now.

More tomorrow...maybe a new scripture!

## Day 17 – Are You Truly Joyful?

*"Joy is not the absence of suffering. It is the presence of God."*

*~Robert Schuller*

If someone asked you are you truly joyful how would you respond?  Well today I am asking and I want your honest answer….not your good little "Christian girl" answer.

Sometimes we have the talk down so well we deceive ourselves.  The most beautiful women I know are truly joyful.  They walk their talk.  They have a peace that oozes from them that makes people want to be with them.  Do you really want to truly change your beautiful?  Then get some joy in our life.

True joy is not based on the size of our jeans, the number on the scale, or whether or not we have a good hair day.  They are circumstances.  Circumstances change like the direction of the wind.  True joy is the presence of God in our life.

He is unchanging.  His presence tames that ugly beast within that tries to tell us we can't be happy in our bodies current state. You know there is nothing wrong with a little holy dissatisfaction with current situations.

In fact an honest evaluation and keen awareness of where you are and where you want to be will be the catalyst for real change in your life but that dissatisfaction should not have a direct link to your joy in life.

So get out an index card….you know the drill.  It's a short one so we will only spend a day on this one.

Write, say, and meditate on the following:

*Be joyful always; pray continually; give thanks in all circumstances, for this is God's will for you in Christ Jesus. ~ 1 Thessalonians 5:16-18*

Did you get that? Joyful ALWAYS. Give thanks in ALL circumstances. Not just when you feel like it or you have exercised or the scale says what you want it to say. All the time.

Journal today about your current level of joy. Pray and ask God help you to find true peace in joy today. What steals your joy? What can you do today to change that? Today is the day for true joy to permeate your heart.

# Day 18 – I'm bored!

*Nobody is bored when he is trying to make something that is beautiful, or to discover something that is true.*

*~William Inge*

I eat a lot when I am bored. Do you? When you were keeping your food journal did you notice that you ate when you were bored? One way to combat this is to do something that makes it difficult to eat while you are doing it i.e. paint your nails, read, etc...

It is very hard to eat chips and read a good book. You don't want to get the pages all greasy and you definitely can't eat with wet nails☺ The point is you need to direct your attention to something other than food.

If you think you want to eat something ask yourself the following questions:

1. Am I thirsty? Drink a glass of water and then reevaluate your hunger.
2. When did I eat last?
3. Am I bored or stressed?

If you ask yourself those questions and realize you really shouldn't be hungry then find an activity. And make it one that you can't eat easily. Not TV watching☺ Be creative. Find something you love and carve out time each day to do it. Work on developing your creative side. Journal, take pictures, scrapbook…etc.

Another thing that will help with the mindless snacking is eating breakfast. People who eat breakfast tend to weigh less and consume less calories during the day. Even if you typically don't like to eat breakfast try eating a little something. Eating a high fiber/ high protein breakfast will be a huge benefit.

# Beauty and the Beast Within

New Verse today....Write it, Say it, Meditate on it!

*I am not saying this because I am in need, for I have learned to be content whatever the circumstances. I know what it is to be in need, and I know what it is to have plenty. I have learned the secret of being content in any and every situation, whether well fed or hungry, whether living in plenty or in want. I can do everything through him who gives me strength. ~ Philippians 4:11-13*

In your journal ask God to fill you with His spirit. Ask Him to continue to reveal to you the reasons for your eating habits. Thank Him for the creativity that He produces in you. Ask Him to teach you the gift of being content.

## Day 19 – Stop The Madness And Save Your Money!

*A blonde is terribly overweight, so her doctor puts her on a diet. "I want you to eat regularly for two days, then skip a day, and repeat this procedure for two weeks. The next time I see you, you'll have lost at least five pounds."*

*When the blonde returns, she's lost nearly 20 pounds. "Why, that's amazing!" the doctor says. "Did you follow my instructions?"*

*The blonde nods. "I'll tell you, though, I thought I was going to drop dead that third day."*

*"From hunger, you mean?" asked the doctor.*

*"No, from skipping."*

Did you know that over 40 billion dollars a year is spent on diet and exercise products? Mind boggling isn't it. Yet the obesity rate in the U.S. continues to rise steadily. It has a lot to do with the instant society we live in. We want results minus the work.

Unfortunately it doesn't work that way and so after we have popped the pills, eaten the cabbage soup, and used the thigh master for about a week we put it away and go back to what we know.

This book is about changing what we know. Becoming educated on how to be healthy and then using all that money to do some good in the world. Can you imagine the impact if people moved more, ate less, and gave the fad fitness and diet money away?

Repeat after me...

I am done spending money on products that promise big results with little or no work. I know that God did not create me to live on cabbage or pills alone.

I know that being healthy is a lifelong commitment that I will pursue diligently without sacrificing joy in my life!

Today clean out your house of this stuff. Throw out the pills, sell the funky cookbooks, and if the exercise equipment is collecting dust put it in the yard sale pile and recoup some of that wasted cash.

Journal today about your feelings on this subject. Have you fallen for any of these fads? How did it make you feel when they didn't work? Make a list of "stuff" you bought in hopes of losing weight and make a commitment to never buy them again.

And while you're at it the next time you're tempted to fall for one of these fads if you truly have the money take it and donate it to a good cause and then eat healthy and go for a walk.

Continue to memorize your scripture!

So what did we learn so far?

- ➢ Slow down!
- ➢ Memorize scripture!
- ➢ Drink water!
- ➢ Move a little more!
- ➢ No more fads!

You got the picture. Keep going girlfriend we are almost to the end! You are doing a fabulous job and let me tell you if you read this and don't lose an ounce but hide God's word in your heart you will feel lighter than you have ever felt in your life!

## Day 20 – Recap!

> *"Motivation is what gets you started.*
> *Habit is what keeps you going."*
> *~Jim Rohn*

It has been a tough topic we have tackled over the last 20 days and whew! I am glad it is coming to an end although I hope you are able to take what you learned and apply it for a lifetime.

I thought I would just quickly sum up some things we have talked about so far and maybe add a few new things for you to process today.

So here goes:

1. **Move more.**
2. **Eat less.**
3. **Drink more water.**
4. **Set realistic goals and be sure your motives are right.** Evaluate, evaluate, evaluate. It is an ongoing process that doesn't stop today. Did you figure out what your triggers are? If not keep looking and praying to get to the root of your bad habits.
5. **Always eat breakfast.** It is a proven fact that thin people and people who maintain weight loss often eat a healthy breakfast.
6. **Eat foods in the most natural state possible.** The less processed the better. I am not saying you need to go on a raw diet but when we eat food the way that God created it we will see many health benefits.
7. **Keep a food journal if you need to.** If you can't lose any weight and you can't seem to figure out why start writing everything down.

I am often blown away when it stares me right in the face and usually all the excuses I had go right in the toilet when I see how much I have been eating.

8. **Reward yourself**.....Not with food though and remember to weigh yourself regularly. Once you reach your goals it is much easier to catch a 5 pound weight gain than a 20.

9. **Remember that we battle things on 3 fronts.** Our flesh, the world, and the Evil one. This just like anything else is a battle and it can be won. You need to wield the sword of the Spirit which is the Word of God. Keep memorizing His word. That will be key to any victory over any stronghold not just your weight.

10. **Once you have lost your weight get rid of your dang "big" clothes.** Don't give yourself the opportunity to wear them again. My wardrobe is very limited in size. I used to keep everything and then I would yo-yo. Now when things get tight I need to do something about it because I don't have my fat clothes to fall back on.

I hope I was able to help and encourage you all in some way. I know it is not easy and I don't want to minimize how great a struggle it can be in our life but I know that through the power of Jesus Christ we can experience victory in any area of our life.

I love you all. Keep journaling and keep memorizing scripture and remember you ARE NOT defined by the tag on your jeans!

## Day 21 – Reflect!

*All excess is rooted in emptiness.*

*~ Beth Moore*

The last day. I don't know if I should laugh or cry. I will probably have a good cry and then go clean my house. I have neglected it quite a bit lately.

Today is about you girlfriend. We are going to spend the day reflecting. Seeking God. Rejoicing in our victory and praying hard about the things that still hold us captive. I hope the end of this book finds you a happier, more confident woman who has a better definition of beautiful than you did 20 days ago.

One last journal entry.

Write about how the above quote makes you feel. Do you agree with it? Do you have any empty places that you are still trying to fill with excess food or excess deprivation and exercise? Often times we spend our whole life in search of the very thing that God is willing to fill for us if we would just ask.

What has been the biggest challenge you have faced in this book? What victories came quickly and easily?

In your times of prayer and journaling and scripture memorization what is the one thing God spoke most often over you? You need to remember this. You need to hold what He says to you tight. If not He will keep teaching you. It's best to just learn it the first time around. Now go look in the mirror. Journal about what you see and feel. Also write your definition of beautiful. Has it changed at all? I hope so.

Final scripture to write, say, and meditate on:

*Your beauty should not come from outward adornment, such as braided hair and the wearing of gold jewelry and fine clothes. Instead, it should be that of your inner self, the unfading beauty of a gentle and quiet spirit, which is of great worth in God's sight. ~ 1 Peter 3:3-4*

So on a final note....You want to be a truly beautiful women then be a servant. Have a gentle and quiet spirit. Be joyful and be thankful in the big things and in the mundane little things of life. Enjoy each new day as if it could be your last and live by the beautiful woman's I Corinthians 13 and love like crazy!

Well that is it my friend. I would love it if you would take a minute and drop me a note and let me know about your journey. Thank you for allowing me to spend this time with you. It has been precious to me.

30710646R00032

Made in the USA
San Bernardino, CA
20 February 2016